Easy to Carry

A small book about poetry with that quick jolt of meaningful inspiration

Edward Rundt

Easy to Carry: A small book about poetry with that quick jolt of meaningful inspiration

Published by TaylorMade Publishing
Jacksonville, FL
www.TaylorMadePublishingFL.com
(904) 323-1334

TaylorMade Publishing

Table of Contents

Introduction..*i*

History of Poetry...*ii*

Type of Poems ....*viii*

Poem List..*1*

Attitude of Gratitude 1

Barbeque...3

Beautiful Sail on the Sea 5

Begin to Forgive 7

Daily Tidbits..9

Defeating Depression 10

Departure From the Comfort Zone 12

Doctor's Office (as a kid)...14

Fluke or Truth..16

God Created Me..17

God Over Ego...19

Good Jingles 21

Have an Umbrella 22

Independence Indeed! 24

Keep Flying Higher..25

Moping in the Mud Pit 27

Never Easy 29

New Additions 31

Persistent Road 33

Responsible, Not a Victim.....................................35

Rhythm and Rhyme 37

Sincere Love 38

Standby or Standup 40

What is a Friend? 42

Why Do I Try?...43

Conclusion..45

About the Author...46

References 47

Introduction

When writing this book, it was my heart's desire to create poems that expressed feelings and emotions everyone has experienced. My goal was to compose a book of poetry that was relatable to all readers.

I was inspired to write poetry by my friend, Aaron Woodson, who has written two poetry books, "The Face of Expression" and "The Face of Expression 2."

I see poetry as a way to tell fables, history, feelings, love, romance, theatrics, sagas, and even as encouragement. As I began to put this book together, I discovered poetry has existed for as long as humans have, which is why I added a section to give a brief history of poetry.

On the pages of this book are my personal experiences, where I share feelings and talk about what I have endured. I hope that through my poems, I can be an inspiration to others and make their lives better.

History of Poetry

When researching poetry, I found an interesting article in the Obsidian, entitled "The History of Poetry" (https://obsidianlit.org/the-history-of-poetry/), from which I learned the following information:

The word "poetry" itself comes from the Greek word poieo meaning "I create," and create it does. People have, and still, use poetry to convey love, lyrics, anger, hate, magic... poetry is a method of creation and manifestation, a method of memory and preservation.

Poetry is an art form, one that predates literacy. Researchers believe that the earliest forms of poetry were passed on as an oral history to the next generation. These were often chants or prayers, but from the physical records left, historical accounts, instructions for everyday activities, and fiction can be counted among the poems. Many early oral histories were told in a poetic notation, likely because the repetition would make it easier to remember.

The trick of using poetry for memory has been practiced for centuries and is still being used today as a mnemonic device. Everyone has likely heard poetry with rhyme schemes like:
- "I before E except after C or when sounding like A as in neighbor or weigh," or...
- "Thirty days hath September, April, June, and November'
  - All the rest have thirty-one,

o   Save February with twenty-eight days clear,
o   And twenty-nine each leap year."

As you can see, poetry is nothing new! According to the Pick Me Up Poetry article "The Historical Timeline of Poetry" (https://pickmeuppoetry.org/the-historical-timeline-of-poetry/) it is easily traced back to what we consider the prehistoric era in which drawings were used to illustrate spiritual stories.

The poetry we are more familiar with today started over 5,000 years ago in Mesopotamia, which would be located today in southern Iraq mainly between the Euphrates and Tigris Rivers (also known as the Fertile Crescent). The oldest known poem today, The Epic of Gilgamesh (2100-1200 BC), was created in Mesopotamia, and it is believed he copied them from earlier works that have been lost or never found for future generations to enjoy.

Poetry further evolved in 400 AD, with the introduction of rhyming couplets and ballads with refrains, which we are familiar with today. During this time, poetry, in addition to art form, was used as a silent form of communication. For example, if a person had been captured by the enemy (or gone into hiding), he or she might leave poems on walls or trees.

Around 1100 AD, it was strongly discouraged to use poetry to express feelings for fear of possible mental problems. In 1500 AD the Renaissance Era emerged. Expressing feelings in poetry became trendy again and even evolved into emphasizing poetry for public performance. In addition to the rekindling of interest in Classical topics, poets also started to write in forms that were not common during the Middle Ages.

For example, they began to use sonnets and other types of poems that had been popularized by Italian poets like Petrarch, who are now known as "sonnet writers." This also led to an interest in developing new poetic meters, which can be seen most prominently today in blank verse poetry but were used regularly at this time. Of course, we cannot forget William Shakespeare, arguably the most famous poet in the world.

Neo-Classical Poetry came about from 1660 to 1800 and brought about a revival of classicalism and poets wanting to explore writing poetry with integrity, which led them back towards more traditional forms like epics, odes, and sonnets instead of experimenting with new styles such as rhyming couplets or free verse. This return also meant that content became more serious once again while prose began exploring topics not seen before within literature, including politics, philosophy, and medicine.

In 1660, England saw the publication of John Dryden's Annus Mirabilis. This poem resulted from the English Restoration and marked a crucial turning point in English literature as it shifted away from Puritanism to more secular themes. The following year marked a significant event for French literature, with Jean Racine publishing his tragedy Phèdre, which helped redefine tragedy in both France and Europe at large. In the years following, French literature continued to evolve.

This period is marked by increasing social unrest, seen in novels like Madame Bovary (1857) and Les Misérables (1862). Around this same time, Charles Dickens' serialization of his novel Oliver Twist began publishing in 1837, with him continuing to contribute more installments until he died in 1870.

Right near the end of the Neo-Classical Poetry came about the Romantic Era, from 1798 to 1850 AD. It was characterized by an emphasis on subjectivity, emotion, spontaneity, and the natural world. The poets of this era were considered to be more accessible than those before them because they wrote about everyday life rather than lofty subjects or themes that were not relatable to most readers.

The Romantics tended to focus on feelings and emotion rather than logic or reason. One of the most famous poets from this era was William Wordsworth, who wrote about the natural world and its connection. He shared these thoughts with Samuel Taylor Coleridge, a fellow poet in Britain at that time. This led them to create what is now known as Lyrical Ballads, which emphasized sensory description and narrative over formal rules or logic.

Finally, the Modern Poetry era started in 1850 and continues today. It is said that Walt Whitman started this era. His works were some of the most innovative and influential poems ever written in

America. This includes "Song of Myself," which has been called one of his best long poems because it captured so much about human nature that nobody had yet expressed before him on paper, such as democratic self-love and acceptance for all types of people, genders, races, and sexualities.

Walt hoped to capture this new sense of democracy through writing in free verse without meter or rhyme – something more akin to prose but still poetic. He also spoke out against slavery during an age where many poets either avoided social issues entirely or wrote platitudes about them.

The first Modernists came to be in the mid-1800s, and they set out to break with many of the established traditions of poetry. The Modernist poets, such as T.S. Eliot (1888-1965) and Ezra Pound (1885-1972), are some of the most prominent writers. The Romanticists who preceded this era wrote about nature and their emotions, whereas the Modernists were interested in exploring more complicated human psychology and society.

As subjects changed for poets, so did their methods of writing poetry. Many would argue that modern poets write with free verse rather than formal rhyme or metered rhythm. These poets sought to use a more conversational voice grounded in lived experience rather than relying on traditional poetic forms or even form at all for their poems. Modern poets also often use other media to present their work, such as in the case of Allen Ginsberg (1926-

1997), who published his poem "Howl" with drawings by William Blake.

As you can see, the Obsidian article "The History of Poetry" (https://obsidianlit.org/the-history-of-poetry/) and the Pick Me Up Poetry article "The Historical Timeline of Poetry" (https://pickmeuppoetry.org/the-historical-timeline-of-poetry/) mention very in-depth history and evolution of poetry that we can enjoy today. In fact, these are popular types of poems written by poets today that I will go over in the "Types of Poems" in the next section.

Type of Poems

The following are the most common types of poems based on the articles: Become a Writer Today article "15 Types of Poems Every Writer Should Know" (https://becomeawritertoday.com/types-of-poems/) and "12 Types of Poems: How to Recognize Them and Write Your Own" (https://www.tckpublishing.com/types-of-poems/)

For this I did my own categorization to provide easier understanding. Bear in mind that each poem does not specifically fall into that one category only.

A. Non-Rhyming

1) Blank Verse: It is commonly without rhyming words but with a strong meter. The words flow well and feel verse-like, even though they don't rhyme. William Shakespeare was a master of blank verse.

2) Ekphrastic do not really have specific rules, but they do speak of another work of art. This term comes from the Greek word for "description." One famous example is found in the "Iliad," where Homer refers to Achilles' shield.

3) Free Verse is a type of poetry that does not rhyme or have a strong meter. It is identified by the short lines and stanzas used to write it. Walt Whitman's "A Noisy, Patient Spider" is an example of free verse.

4) Haiku: Japanese poetry form that doesn't rhyme which has 3 lines:
   - 1st line = 5 syllables
   - 2nd line = 7 syllables
   - 3rd line = 5 syllables

B. Patterned or Rhyming

1) Ballad: Traditionally a song, a ballad is a type of poem that uses rhymed quatrains, or four lines grouped together, to tell a story. Bob Dylan is a modern example of a ballad writer.

2) Concrete Poetry is designed to take a particular shape or form on the page. Poets can manipulate spacing or layout to emphasize a theme or important element in the text, or sometimes they can take the literal shape of their subjects. For example, "The Altar" by George Herbert was intended to resemble a church altar.

3) Epigram is a short and sweet, usually witty, poem that is nothing more than a couplet or quatrain. Benjamin Franklin's phrase, "Little strokes fell great oaks," is an example of an epigram.

4) Limerick is typically a humorous five-line poem. It uses an AABBA rhyming pattern. The first line, second line and fifth line of a limerick have seven to ten syllables and rhyme, while the third and fourth lines have five to seven syllables and rhyme.

5) Lyric Poetry shows feelings and emotion. It may use rhyming verse or free form, but it is distinct from epic and narrative poetry because the focus is not on a story, but on a feeling. Most Shakespearean sonnets are examples of lyric poetry.

6) Rhymed Poetry focuses on rhyming words at the end of each line or couplet.

7) Sonnets are poems with 14 lines that contain a specific rhyme scheme and meter. There are various types of rhyming schemes that can be used in sonnets, and typically sonnets have 10 syllables per line. One of the most famous sonnet writers was Shakespeare, but Italian poet Francesco Petrarch, creator of the Petrarchan sonnet, and English poet Elizabeth Barrett Browning were also prominent. A famous example of rhymed poetry or a sonnet is Browning's "Sonnet Number 43."

8) Villanelle is a highly specific type of poetry. This 19-line poem has five tercets, or groups of five lines, and a quatrain. The famous Dylan Thomas poem, "Do Not Go Gentle Into That Good Night" shows the Villanelle type of poetry.

C. Narrative

1) Elegies are poems with themes of mourning and loss. Walt Whitman's "O Captain! My Captain!" is a famous example of an elegy mourning the death of Abraham Lincoln.

~ X ~

2) Epic is a long poem that tells a story, typically about great heroes, either real or fiction. These poems may not rhyme, though they can. Homer's "Iliad" and "Odyssey" are two commonly known epics.

3) Epitaph is much like an elegy, only shorter. Epitaphs commonly appear on gravestones, but they can also be humorous. There are no specific rules for epitaphs or their rhyme schemes.

4) Ode pays homage or tribute to a subject, but it may be less serious than an elegy. One of the most famous odes is John Keats' "Ode on a Grecian Urn."

5) Narratives are like epics in that they tell a story, but they are not as long and often not as heroic. The famous "The Road Not Taken" by Robert Frost is an example of a short narrative poem.

Attitude of Gratitude

I started out with this poem because it is easy to take things for granted. This is especially true with living in the United States, having access to so many privileges. From ordering a sandwich, having my car serviced, traffic lights working correctly, and being able to express my feelings openly without that absolute fear of reprisal, my privileges abound. When saying grace, I say it is a privilege to have what I have, since there are many who only dream of these luxuries.

It is easy to employ the use of the word gratitude
in a loose way
Gratitude is more than a mere word
It is about an attitude, knowing that blessings are a privilege
not as a means of leverage
It alludes to being thankful for the bounty that we have
This also encompasses gratefulness
that helps us truly be great
The Latin word *gratus* is the root word for gratitude
which also means to appreciate,
and I also find that gives me true status
Gratitude constitutes a love that is not easy to repay
At this point the best thing is to persist

and pray to find accord with the Lord.
So that can you have the
attitude of gratitude.

Barbeque

A simple fun way to have a gathering with friends and family, whether for a special occasion, vacation, or just a nice meal, is doing a barbeque. I find this especially true from mid-spring, summer, and early autumn in most parts of the world. With me living in Florida, a barbeque can practically be done in all seasons.

What I find great about a barbeque is that it can be done for a purpose or even if there isn't really a reason. All that is required is a good grill, either charcoal or a burner with propane tank, cooking utensils, pans to cook in, and getting good food to cook in the first place. Look at that, something that simple can make a day memorable! Now that is a cuisine to cook in an open fire!

We have many differences and argue,
but I say we can agree that we love having
that good barbeque.
The succulent scent of the cooking meat with
that tasty sauce and seasoning
that makes it the right combination.
On that nice summer evening that is such a sensation.
For me, I hope the one cooking also chose to add in corn, carrots,
squash, and potatoes.
Then that infamous call of "come and get it"
that motivates me to get to that table and immediately sit.

After everyone is in place
then comes the moment to show our appreciation
by saying grace.
Such a treat
whether we are with or without
others to have that feast to eat.
Well, as far as I am concerned
I think we can all agree
that barbeque would be for you and for me.
Having a chance to eat such a good meal
is a good big deal.

Beautiful Sail on the Sea

Daydreaming can be a nice break from the daily grind but must be done carefully. It can be used to set goals when used correctly. When daydreaming becomes a way to escape or anesthetize your problems then this becomes bad. Coping with the problem is okay if you don't have the means to resolve the problem, but that is much like having to be on a lifeboat or, worse, a life preserver if your ship sinks. We must discern when we have to cope or take action, as the Serenity Prayer goes.

God, grant me the serenity
to accept the things I cannot change,
the courage to change the things I can,
and the wisdom to know the difference.
Living one day at a time, enjoying one moment at a time;
accepting hardship as a pathway to peace, taking as Jesus did
this sinful world as it is, not as I would have it, trusting that you
will make all things right if I surrender to your will; so that I
may be reasonably happy in this life and supremely happy with
you in the next.

Next time you watch a movie or read a biography about victory, remember the work and agony that took place in between.

At one time or another we wish we had that extra dime
to live in paradise with just that lucky roll of the dice.

Reality though requires us to know that we will end up getting
stuck if we think that we can just go by luck.
Fairytales and fables merely say "Happily Ever After"
but we know that we only get the happy conclusion
if we are willing and able.
A happy conclusion that comes to my mind
is to be in that beautiful boat sailing in the sea.
This is so picturesque, yet I realize it will require
working at that boring office desk.
To keep that sailboat, it must be
locked onto a dock.
Then upkeep is needed so the beautiful boat
does not become a heap
that will only creak and leak.
Aggravation, agitation, and frustration
arise when I think about this.
After a moment though,
if I fail to do the hardships to upkeep
my ship then I will never see
that beautiful sail on the sea.

Begin to Forgive

The popular theme in today's entertainment is the protagonist, hero or even anti-hero, being able to fulfill their desires by exercising their rage of revenge on their perpetrators, or especially those who betrayed them. Endings portrayed by the protagonist achieving their vengeance-based goals with great rewards are common. Of course, then vendettas and revenge seem more appealing.

Then I remembered an uncle of mine (retired police chief) who told me that life is a two-way street. Fantasy ensnares us to believe that vengeance is an easy-to-access medium with only exclusive access for us. Reality dictates that anyone with capability and determination can exercise vengeance. Most likely this becomes a vicious cycle of misery and can, at the worst, turn into a horrible and, even, deadly escalation.

Whenever I think of someone who has wronged me,
that makes me livid.
Then I hear someone say
that I must forgive.
I first think and even say that it is crazy
that if I do that then that would be retreat
and more that I must give.
Goes to show how it is easy in human nature

it seems so great to hate.
Which first is sweet as candy
that makes it easy to embrace.
The trap has been set to instead handicap me
with misery locking me in that nasty brace.
Foolishly thinking that speaking my mind to openly say
to put my feelings on that falsely bold display.
Becoming gullible to think beating
that wrongdoer to a pulp will bring resolve.
The vicious cycle of misery
got me wrapped in the trap.
Unwittingly taking what I hated darkened my heart
and is becoming a part of me.
Now I am here, stuck on that nasty ride
on my raging vehicle of false pride,
simultaneously being ripped apart by fear.
Then God gives me a strong gentle rap,
saying if you want to end the misery,
then please grab onto my holy strap.
Thank you, God, for lifting me up,
helping me to see that when I forgive that misery,
I no longer must live in it.
Learning to forgive is not forgetting,
but refusing to give into hate.
Thanks to God who gives me the conviction
to give misery the notice of eviction.

Daily Tidbits

In doing my readings as a poet in different places, I encounter good people. Recently, I befriended a woman who is a real estate agent and I found it joyful to speak with her.

Dealing with selling and buying homes can be very tricky and isn't always a steady business. She keeps memes to help motivate her each day, to keep steadfast and not let frustration get the better of her.

Always strive to be amazing.
Otherwise, mediocrity will drive me crazy.
If it is in God's will, I can do anything.
A prayer to God is better than a social media ping.
I can always choose to be positive
which is the progressive vector to victory.
Be grateful to celebrate God's gift
of my distinctive individuality.
Anything else is just a foolish idiosyncrasy.
Nothing is guaranteed, except never trying
absolutely does not lead you to succeed.

Defeating Depression

Sadness is a not so pleasant emotion that we have. It is often mixed in with depression that gives us melancholy, which is not an ally. This is commonly caused by the loss of a loved one, a relationship that is done, especially with no explanation, or something that we grudgingly do as a necessity.

Starting with the letter "D," depression and draining go hand in hand. Oh, that extra effort it seems we must ask of ourselves to accomplish a mere task. Just as these chains feel heavy, we must make that task to find whatever that bar is to break these same chains so that we no longer must endure that ridiculous pain.

Oh, those rainy days
when it is emotionally draining.
The times when I have no choice
other than to endure subjection to rejection.
Making me feel oppression
that leads to depression.
Knocking me down
and telling me that I am only a clown.
In those moments it seems that
I will remain in a cage.
After reminiscing, I know if I do not rise back up
that I will only become more bitter with age.

Remembering that after rain and gloom,
the sun will shine again and
the flowers will blossom.
Always remember, taking the courageous steps
will lead to a feeling of awesomeness.

Departure From the Comfort Zone

It is everywhere on the news! There are protests and rallies for groups and people fighting for their rights. The feelings are so passionate that sometimes it seems that it is done in spite of the weather. Whether at home or abroad, the fight for rights is a cry for freedom. From a pardon, permission to do something or even those who seek a new kingdom, that freedom is universal and relatable.

Too often freedom is misunderstood, and the term is even abused by those with selfish agendas. I think to grasp and experience freedom in its right form is to first understand what freedom is all about.

Our comfort zone is comparable to the
safe haven for the mariners.
It is good when there are storms, or
we are dealing with troubles and disparagers.
Nice a safe haven is to avoid the stress
of being in distress.
Our zone of comfort is nice
since there is no need to confront the unknown.
No fear to fail in what eventually
becomes our jail that prevents us to go.

The Temptations song "Cloud Nine" says
how nice it is since we have no responsibility.
The price is that I am giving
someone a part of me.
What we call the *Comfort Zone*
makes us think we can just isolate.
Please learn that it is a mistake
before it is too late.
To chase dreams does take planning and time
but do not just sit and wait.
Before you know it, the opportunities will pass
in a flash which makes it too late.
It is understandable to fear the unknown
of what you have not done before.
Do not continue to only pace the same old floor
and find the courage to open another door
since you never know that something special is in store.
Often it is easy to remain in our *Comfort Zone*
since there is so much good.
Eventually it can keep us from being great and
end up saying the cliché statement of
could've, would've, should've.

Doctor's Office (as a kid)

Right now, I am in the waiting room to see the doctor to validate my aches and pains. To make sure that this is not serious and can be quickly fixed. Looking back at when I was a kid, it was nice to miss school when I was sick, but then came going to the doctor and dreading that shot.

Gladly, I am an adult and can look back to know that getting that shot is nothing more than the quick pinprick that brings the cure.

Here I sit because I got sick.
Well, that can happen to anyone at any clock's tick.
My momma tells me it is going to be all right.
After hearing that I may get a shot,
as a kid I think, yeah right.
The illness and the anxiety that the shot will hurt
make me feel discomfort.
As a kid I think, oh I hate to be in the waiting room.
Then as the door creaks and opens,
oh this gives me the creeps.
The nervousness looms
as I am brought to a room.
As the doctor walks in it occurs to him
that I am sick and unsure.
With a mix of candor and kindness

the doctor takes time to make me feel assured.
Tells me I will have to get a shot,
which will momentarily cause a pain.
Eventually it will help me a lot and
the cure I will gain.
The doctor then takes the needle to stick
me with that temporary pinprick.
Looking back, I am glad that I was brave
so that I no longer have to remain sick.

Fluke or Truth

Discerning truth and lies is not easy. Sometimes first knowing the truth is not always pleasing. Lies are fun and mischievous and prevent you from true achievement and a life that is not adventurous. Inspired by the popular phrase and game "Truth or Dare," there comes my poem "Fluke or Truth." Yes, that is its name.

Based on the need to be aware of the con-artists,
thieves, scammers, and those who abuse.
To help me discern, the question "Fluke or Truth?"
is what I use.
Even the Bible warns the devil has the ability and guise to
impersonate an angel of light as it's disguise.
Also remember to test every spirit because the devil definitely
does not have your best interest.
Flukes are pieces of facts with sugarcoating
to complete its lies.
Truth may not be delightful and it can taste bitter,
but it does not require a disguise.
This may sound cynical but know that if something sounds too
good to be true then it likely is not true,
then being vigilant will hold you together like glue.

God Created Me

There are many times that we feel inadequate when looking at others. Seemingly we were not the cream of the crop; therefore, our self-esteem was not at the top. When we read a magazine, search the internet, or watch TV and see the stars seemingly make looking and doing good so easy.

Thankfully the world is not entirely comprised of images. In fact, you would find that those strutting on the catwalk, owning the big shows that talk, or exhibiting on the big screen are often the ones who seek esteem the most. Well, that seems to be so odd, until I remember that the source of esteem is truly from God.

What makes this wonderful is to have that incorruptible, unchanging, and everlasting source that I can always rely on when my situation(s) in this world aren't so good or even go very turbulent. Many times I wish I were that famous athlete with the talent to flair and flaunt, but that can be stopped by old age or injuries. Sometimes, too, I wish I was that multi-billionaire with lots of cash, and then I realize that the economy and currency value can change in a flash.

My mother often tells me that the day I was born
there were many who adored me.
I had to first learn how to walk

then learn how to talk.
When growing up I was not
the cool one in school.
Sometimes there were those who considered me
more of a dud than a stud.
Yes, the curtness of others
sometimes did hurt.
No, it was not fair yet I do not know how
but I never despaired.
Even though I did not know God personally, I always
had that feeling there was a reason He created me.
I say this easily because I found
that drive to strive.
With a lot of help from my friend and Savior Jesus,
He helped me keep my grip to face the hardships.
Thank you, Jesus, for it is no mere
coincidence that I am here
You know that I still question You but
then see that you created me to do a quest.

God Over Ego

Saying that I know God created me for a purpose makes the reason for writing this poem self-explanatory. Simply put, I must give credit to God because it is due and it is true.

Yes, I do forget to put my ego in check, but it is God Who helps me with that. Otherwise basing my life on my volatile ego would make life feel like a madhouse.

It is that ego of mine that makes me think
that I can smoothly flow.
Therefore, there are many bad places
that I want to go.
Yes, that ego that eggs me on
to go towards that gratification.
Because I think I can gain
that quick validation.
Oh, that feeling is as sweet as candy
that seems to come in handy.
After satisfying that craving,
then later I think what I did was crazy.
Suddenly I feel that built up guilt.
Why do this just for that momentary bliss.
When will I learn so that next time I will not burn.
Well, guess what, right now I can begin to learn

that the ego lies.
Realize that it is God,
not the ego I must strive for.
Knowing that Jesus will always ride with me and
for my sins on the cross that he did die for me.
Thinking about it hard enough, I found out
that ego can be an acronym for Easing God Out.
Yes, the ego can give me a temporarily good fun
but with the steep cost of striking out.
It is human nature to think
that God is odd.
Eventually, it is foolish to listen to the ego
and forego Jesus.

Good Jingles

Looking back on the years, I find that I can remember commercials with the same level of joyfulness as a cartoon, TV show or a movie. There is something about advertisement that can be relatable with people from diverse backgrounds.

Even decades later, there are still commercials and ads that continue to be talked about and enjoyed, even by those from younger generations.

So simple is a single jingle
It seems nothing like a quick fling but so unforgettable
Easy to remember and sticks to me forever
Sometimes there is nothing like a good jingle
For advertisers use it to help sell their angle
It is a good simple jingle that is so memorable
I think of that Wendy's "Where's the Beef"
commercial by Clara Peller
She was so good that I cheered and
yelled "Yeah you tell 'em!"
Who can forget the Life cereal commercial with little Mikey
His brothers had him try that cereal and then they said,
"He Likes it; Hey Mikey!"

Have an Umbrella

Rotterdam, The Netherlands was my first duty station while serving in the U.S. Army. The quickest way to describe Rotterdam is that it is the European twin to Seattle, Washington. Yeah, as you may have gathered, it rains a lot.

When my commanding offer gave me the initial briefing speech, it was the usual keep my military bearing and be vigilantly sober. He then closed his speech by telling me there are many great places to see and a lot of wonderful people to meet, so since it rains a lot, just invest in good rain gear and an umbrella so that you can have a great experience here.

Life can be unpredictable like the weather.
Even with today's technology those forecasts carry
about as much weight as a feather.
Oh no, you cannot tell whether it will be rain or shine.
That is when I must know to say oh well,
keep moving and I will end up being more than fine.
Someone told me there are many sites to see, make new friends
with fellas and fall in love with girls that are fine.
He said that if it rains just open your umbrella.
So, on that first rainy day I did that, and this was as wonderful as
a song done in acapella.
Yes, enduring the rain I am saying oh it is such a pain.

As momma said, "You cannot get angry at the weather."
I take that advice and know now that having that umbrella helps
me enjoy life, which is getting ahead of the weather.

Independence Indeed!

Our great nation of the United States has its foundation built on independence. That is what makes being a U.S. citizen so wonderful. This is an inspiration for my poem below.

The word "Independence" for us it strongly resonates,
since this is a word that we can be proud to state.
Opposite word is dependence, which carries no status,
yet it is an easy action that can be done by any of us.
We can sadly sit on the fence's edge since we do not have to take
sides and this requires no courage.
Easy to remember to July 4th, 1776, our forefathers
made the Declaration of Independence,
but never forget how hard it was to stay that stance.
Today, the 4th of July is seen by many as a time
to party and be merry but never forget those who
fought through the times that were scary.
Next time you see the colorful fireworks in flight
let us remember those who gave it their all
for our independence fight.
Remember the courage, fight and good deeds
that allow all of us to still proudly cry
"Independence Indeed."

Keep Flying Higher

As a military veteran, I look back on my days of service with the Army. A valuable lesson I learned is, despite the different branches of the military, we all serve a critical purpose to fight for the American flag "Old Glory." Just that itself makes a good story!

Additionally, I also remember the Van Halen song "Dreams" done in tribute to the U.S. Navy's Blue Angels, how that also resonated great positive emotions. Even today that holds true for me, which I still keep in mind when I feel down.

This morning I feel the aches and their oppression
during a lapse garnished with depression.
Along with its cousin spawning from fatigue called frustration,
I still go through the motions.
Partially I do this out of vain
since my pride does not want
to be taken down by pain.
Eventually I start to lose my dosage of adrenaline and
momentum then exhaustion kicks in.
After I sit and ponder
then my minds start to wander.
Feeling frustrations tirade of tears though my eyes,
yet still I know those are lies.
Knowing the naysayers are grinning,

this gets my mind churning.
Then out of nowhere come the memories of
Memorial Day, 4th of July, Labor Day, and Veterans' Day
and seeing the Blue Angels fly above,
which brings happiness back in play.
Now I scream,
not in pain but in joy thinking about
Van Halen's 1986 hit song "Dreams."
Paraphrasing the lyrics to first know that even
in a world with challenges so strong
that I am most definitely worthy to belong.
Then the song finishes off that it is good to depend
on dreams because that is what love
is made of in the end.
I give the words of encouragement to start
drying the tears you have cried,
get back up and get back to flying higher.

Moping in the Mud Pit

After high school and a couple years of college, I worked at a furniture store as a warehouse worker. The job itself was okay, with low end pay checks to boot. What made me despise this job was being around others who liked to party, were lazy, or who I would call the dead weights.

To me it is the dead weights that are the worst. I define dead weights as people with no ambition who will even go as far as to sabotage any advancements and improvements you make in life.

In this experience of my life, that is where I was inspired to use the term "mud pit" because while they seem like fun for a short moment, it is a filthy place that you can even get stuck in, like quicksand.

Each day it is another twirl
for me in the real world.
To do more toil in the soil so that I can plant the seeds
and later harvest the results of my good deeds.
Being in the dirt of life can easily make me think
I am stuck in a mud pit.
Yes, it then becomes that trap of misery and
throwing a party to cynically celebrate pity.
Well stop right there because life can be unfair,

then again life also can be fair.
Therefore, lets step back and know that our mud pit
is negativity's henchman called
misery nagging you where you sit.
Think about how pigs see mud pits
as nature's coolers.
Know that mud pits are still used for
construction by builders.
Our moping in the mud pit is misery
making us sick...sincerely!
Do not just be angry and shout,
but keep working little by little to get out.
It is okay if we get stuck for a day,
but we do not have to wallow and stay.
Naysayers will say
just forget about it and let us play.
God tells us to forego the players, forge forward,
grab my hand, so that we know that in this bondage
we do not have to remain.

Never Easy

It is so cavalier to be that someone who has that caviar, not always for the taste of food but just to have that sweet status.

I want to stay in that stratosphere of Cloud Nine because that would feel so divine. Then I am reminded that it takes that tough turbulent climb. I cannot deny that I do not always want to make that tough climb, but sadly for me there is the law of gravity. It states that it is easier to go down than it is to stay up.

We love something that comes with ease because
it's that fun tease that immediately pleases us.
Later comes regret for not saying no to cheap comfort
rather than taking the courage to confront.
Those who make the news…
do not take the easy snooze
are willing to endure the toils
rather than take the easy spoils
never lose hope even
when everyone else says "Nope"
find ways to shine
when it is much easier to whine
not afraid to fail
despite those who would leave us and bail
Greatness comes when you find courage

to endure the sleaze, not the ease, of life.
Achievement consists of commencement
with an ongoing commitment
and a strong dash of effort
without forfeit.
Ironically, achievement requires the
following antonyms to…
abandon the toxic people who hold you ransom
depart from bad habits that tear you apart
destroy the factors that drain your joy
forfeit the games that people play
that restrict you like a corset
The road to success is never easy with the destination of the
pleasing achievement.

New Additions

As we live through life, we notice that change is a definite constant. Whether we like it or not, change is here to stay. I have not always liked change, especially when I was younger, since I did not want to leave that "comfort zone" where I had success and seemed to be a winner. Later, after going through the change that I did not necessarily want, I looked back at that period in the cocoon of comfort and saw how small and limited I really was. A sign of my maturity is to embrace the meaningful losses over the meaningless victories.

Well, we may not always have victories and defeats in our daily life, but we have experiences. A more subtle example of a new addition is trying a new cuisine, learning a different style of exercise, taking that new dance lesson. It has been proven that trying new things helps our body functions work better over time. Eating new foods provides our body with additional nutrients and learning new skills makes our brain work better.

Sometimes it is the fear of the unknown
that prevents us to grow.
For fear is not something to cheer about.
It does get easy to moan
while sitting in our comfort zone.
In our bitterness it is easy to say

oh golly and feel sorry.
Those are the things that condition
us not to want that nice new addition.
Know this that it would be foolish
to miss something lavish.
Do not be afraid because that new
thing just might end up being great.
Step out and ascend since that
is the only way to find excellence.
Then again you may not like that new thing but
that is still better than to be that bitter sitter.

Persistent Road

In the many years that I have lived, there are so many books, stories, news items and movies that are based on persistence.

It is such a glorious subject to base many plots on that is enjoyed repetitively by many. This holds especially true with rags to riches and fat to fit based stories. The part that separates the spectators from the achievers is how persistently they forego the quick pleasures of life.

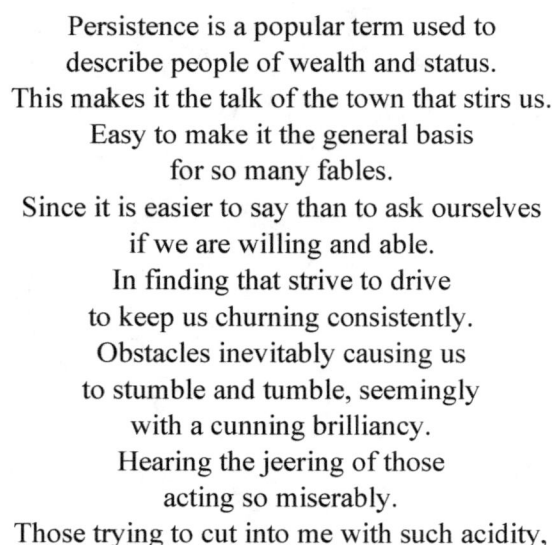

Persistence is a popular term used to
describe people of wealth and status.
This makes it the talk of the town that stirs us.
Easy to make it the general basis
for so many fables.
Since it is easier to say than to ask ourselves
if we are willing and able.
In finding that strive to drive
to keep us churning consistently.
Obstacles inevitably causing us
to stumble and tumble, seemingly
with a cunning brilliancy.
Hearing the jeering of those
acting so miserably.
Those trying to cut into me with such acidity,

yes, again it is those naysayers.
Please backseat warriors, repeat your inferior sayings,
and enrage me to be the dragon slayer.
Right now, I moan and groan, but no thank you I will stay on
that treacherous yet bestowed Persistent Road.
I have been on the short end of the dangers
and endured the many days and nights of anger.
Despite that, I refuse to freeload
off brothers or let others cause me to
give in and implode.
Instead, I still choose to pray to God and say,
"Please reload me and help me uphold
that righteous code."
Because at the end of that tough spell
the consistent persistence will make me shine and
glow which will bode well.

Responsible, Not a Victim

We all have moments when we unexpectedly get wronged or robbed. Sometimes that opponent is just too strong to stop them from taking advantage of you. It is maddening and enraging to think of that defeat repeatedly. Yet I know that I can stay down, pout and cry victim or I can get back up for another bout to shout victory.

For this poem, one source of inspiration is the Eagles classic song "Victim of Love" which is about a woman who is in love with a bad man, in part because it gives her that thrill in which there is a price to pay.

Every day someone gets robbed, cheated, or even murdered.
To say that they are a victim then gets murmured.
These cases of victimhood are legit.
Yes, that I understand and completely get.
Sadly, many use the term loosely.
Especially when one is irresponsible and acts foolishly.
In turn, in what toys
do we foolishly think we can find joy?
When we play with fire and fail
it is easy to call others a liar and
run to somebody to help us bail.
Guess what, those foolish tales

just will not sail.
Therefore, stop being gullible to use the idiotic idiom,
Oh I am a victim, and find the courage to be responsible
Let us face it, at least a certain amount of pleasure,
profit, and personal safety will be gone.
Eventually, taking courage to being responsible
will give us both legs to stand on.

Rhythm and Rhyme

After listening to a good friend of mine do her musical concert, I thought of how I enjoyed listening to her performance. Sometimes it is a simple song that brings good thoughts and joy.

The melody of the music is such a sweet sound to my ear.
I find that to be the cure of my melancholy.
The tweets and the songs that I hear are so sweet.
What I enjoy the most is a rhythm that
gives the song reasoning.
Added with the rhyme to the song much
like what is food with seasoning.
I love to hear the rhymes
that wash away the daily grime.
Repetitively, I simply ask to find that rhythm
since it is that musical algorithm.
Because it is like that toy
that gives me joy.

Sincere Love

As do most people, I long for that sincere and meaningful love. Having lived long enough in this world, love is way more than romance. The truest form of love is supporting and selfless. Love exists not only in the romance of a beautiful woman with whom I long to dance.

The presence of love is with those who will stand with you during the bad days. It helps overcome the fair-weather fans.

Sincere love is truly found amongst those who band with me for support. This is like giving me those boxing gloves to punch through the obstacles and opponents of life.

For I have longed for love
that fits like a glove
giving peace like a dove.
There have been many dances
with prance that advertise romance.
Yet, I find true joy when I can make you smile
even if more than a mile
away since there is no guile.
Then I can say "Oh Boy"
with sincere joy
and do not need to be coy.

I simply am grateful,
no need to be grandiose nor boast.
It gives that power to reassure
that overcomes hardships pressure.
There is nothing that has the soft caress
and yet will prevent you from dismal regress.

Standby or Standup

A popular expression I have heard in the past decade is "Are You a Fan or a Follower?" The meaning I have learned from this is as follows. Now a fan only watches and cheers as something progresses through. The follower is the fan that will stick with it through thick and thin and even contribute their dimes and time.

Taking these concepts and applying them to those who are spectators that standby to watch the news and the courageous ones who make the effort to standup and be good news.

Whenever we watch television
or search the internet,
there is so much news that makes us envision.
From facts, achievements, tragedy, opinion polls
and other information about those bickering,
and all that right at our beck and call.
So easy to sit and standby and use in social circles
since we think everything is at our disposal.
That easy jitter and jargon that we can cook up on
social media like Facebook or Twitter.
It is nice to know the news especially when something bad does
not happen in our back yard or pad.
Suddenly when we endure clamor
then we see how meaningless the chatter was.

Let this be a reminder for us to prioritize
our lives to act and not be overcome by distraction.
Stop talking so much smack
and get back on track
since finding traction
will lead us to better satisfaction.

What is a Friend?

Too many times in our lives, we encounter many who are insincere or even dangerous to our well-being. Especially living in today's world where scammers and con artists are looming, perhaps even more dangerously than before, we have to ask how to decipher who is a foe and who is a friend.

What is a friend?
For starters, I will say it is greater than a trend!
When under pressure does not bend.
Does not try to be slick with you nor pull a trick
Will be as direct as a high kick.
A friend will never hurt you or treat you like dirt.
Even in the bad times one will stay near and remain sincere.
Because it is the norm
for a friend to help be the anchor for your storms.
For a friend is the basis of a true lover who you endear and will consider you dearly.
After all, you cannot say boyfriend and
girlfriend without friend.
A friend is great because they will stay until the end.
Which brings that very fragrance with
the sweet taste of a strawberry.

Why Do I Try?

There are many days that I feel such agony, depression, and frustration that I even struggle to get out of bed. In those moments of anxiety when I do not want to depart from the comfort of my mattress, peel away that protective shell of my sheets, and remain looking at my phone to provide my social media.

Shortly, though, it occurs to me that my sense of comfort is limited because then I will not be able to enjoy that nice warm cup of java, soak up the sun, have a delicious meal, do a dance with a beauty queen, or be able to enjoy my hobbies.

That is when I truly find the courage, wake up and tell myself that I must try. With that I have invented that mathematic formula of encouragement:

0 tries = 100% failure
Success = # of failures + 1 more try

For the days of frustration, when I cry
and ask myself why even try when …
Friends turned out to be fiends
Vacations making me feel vacated
Things getting me feeling beaten instead of better
Romances that looked like love ended up getting lost
Reminiscing on this causes me to cry

and ask why even bother to try because
it is futile, that causes me to tire.
Inexplicitly then comes those divine sparks
which rekindles that fire that fuels the fight.
The burning of that fire
then restarts that yearning of desire
and to gain that once lost might.
Suddenly realizing that if I quit
then all I will do is sit
forever just crying,
asking why instead of trying.
Let us rebound from the frivolous pits
and climb back up the peaks of mount ambitious.
Those many failures to success are merely
mediocrity's lure that traps you to comfortably sit,
easily quit and end up merely just crying and asking why.
Remember that success is to try once more
plus, the quote, unquote, failures of the past
that you have taken the courage to overcome.

Conclusion

These poems have covered many subjects of our lives. In many of the poems, there are the following recurring themes of…

The not-so-good and even darker episodes of our lives
that we must fight through to write happier chapters.
Dreams and achievements will only happen
with persistence and hard work.
Life can be wonderful with
being positively realistic.

With courage, planning, effort and persistence, good things are gained to make our desires become our reality.

About the Author

Edward Rundt was born in Willoughby, Ohio in 1971. He grew up in Mentor, Ohio, where he graduated from high school and attended college for a couple of years.

In 1991 he moved to Schenectady, NY to live with his mother and stepfather. He worked in a furniture store warehouse for two years.

In 1993, Edward chose to serve in the U.S. Army, both for his country and to better himself. He retired honorably from the U.S. Army in 2013, after serving 20 years. During his service, Edward was stationed in Europe, Qatar, Kuwait, South Korea, Afghanistan, and several states in the continental U.S., plus Alaska.

Edward then transitioned to the Information Technology (IT) field working for companies such as Home Depot, Florida Blue, Bossanova Robotics, and Bank of America.

Edward now resides in Jacksonville, Florida where he wrote this poetry book, his first work of literature. He plans to continue his writing journey.

References

[1]. 12 Types of Poems: How to Recognize Them and Write Your Own. (2019, June 17). TCK Publishing. https://www.tckpublishing.com/types-of-poems/

[2]. Göke, N. (2020, September 16). The 7 Kinds of True Freedom. Medium. https://ngoeke.medium.com/the-7-kinds-of-true-freedom-cfdecef2cc86

[3]. H, N. (2021, June 22). 15 Types of Poems Every Writer Should Know. Becomeawritertoday.com. https://becomeawritertoday.com/types-of-poems/

[4]. The History of Poetry. (2018, April 24). Obsidian. https://obsidianlit.org/the-history-of-poetry/

[5]. The Historical Timeline of Poetry: 5000BC- Present – Pick Me Up Poetry. (n.d.). https://pickmeuppoetry.org/the-historical-timeline-of-poetry/

[6]. Woodson, A. (2018). The Face of Expression. Author House.

[7]. Woodson, A. (2020). The Face of Expression 2: In Your Face. TaylorMade Publishing LLC of Florida.